Celebrating
PASSOVER

by Diane Hoyt-Goldsmith
photographs by Lawrence Migdale

Holiday House / New York

This book is dedicated to our grandparents,
great-grandparents, and great-great-uncles and aunts,
who have given us their names
to honor and remember them by,
and who have loved us and taught us to celebrate life,
and to honor our Jewish traditions
from generation to generation.

—Jenna, Micah, and Jared Kamrass

Library of Congress Cataloging-in-Publication Data
Hoyt-Goldsmith, Diane.
    Celebrating Passover / by Diane Hoyt-Goldsmith; photographs by Lawrence Migdale.
        p. cm.
    Includes index.
    Summary: Uses one family's celebration of Passover to describe the religious significance,
    traditions, customs, and symbols of this Jewish holiday.
    ISBN 0-8234-1420-5 (hardcover)
    1. Passover—Juvenile literature. 2. Seder—Juvenile literature. [1. Passover. 2. Seder] I. Migdale, Lawrence, ill. II. Title.

BM695.H3 H695 2000
296.4'37—dc21   99-049006

Acknowledgments
We would like to thank Rabbi Lewis Kamrass and his wife, Renee, as well as their children, Micah, Jenna, and Jared, for inviting us to celebrate Passover in their home and for sharing their traditions with us. We are grateful for the enthusiastic participation of all the grandparents, David and Anna Lee Kamrass, and Alvin (Zayde) and Vivian (Bubby) Slotin.

    We are also grateful for help in the early stages of our project from Rabbi Sam Joseph of Cincinnati, Ohio, and Rabbi Peretz Wolf-Prusan of San Francisco, California. We appreciate the helpful cooperation of the staff at the Isaac M. Wise Temple in Cincinnati, Ohio. Thanks also to Noni Rudavsky of the Dalsheimer Rare Book Room in the Library of the Hebrew Union College–Jewish Institute of Religion in Cincinnati, Ohio, for all her help and advice.

    The passages on pages 14 and 15 are from *The Torah: The New JPS Translation According to the Traditional Hebrew Text.* Copyright © 1962 by the Jewish Publication Society. Used by permission.

    The Haggadah used by the family for their Passover celebration is *A Passover Haggadah*, The New Union Haggadah prepared by the Central Conference of American Rabbis, and published by Grossman Publishers, a division of Viking/Penguin, in 1974. Excerpts on pages 20 and 23 are used with permission.

    The Haggadah (HUC.MS.444) pictured on page 8 is shown courtesy of the Klau Library at the Hebrew Union College–Jewish Institute of Religion in Cincinnati, Ohio. It is a fifteenth century manuscript from Germany, attributed to the copiest and illuminator Meier Jeffie.

Micah enjoys riding his bike in his neighborhood.

The Hebrew calendar is a lunar calendar. Its months are based on the phases of the moon. Each time a new moon appears, a new month begins.

Tishri	Sept.–Oct.
Heshvan	Oct.–Nov.
Kislev	Nov.–Dec.
Tevet	Dec.–Jan.
Shevat	Jan.–Feb.
Adar	Feb.–Mar.
Nisan	Mar.–Apr.
Iyar	Apr.–May
Sivan	May–June
Tammuz	June–July
Av	July–Aug.
Elul	Aug.–Sept.

Micah is nine years old. He lives in Cincinnati, Ohio, where it is spring and time for the baseball season to begin. Micah looks forward to watching the Cincinnati Reds play.

Springtime is special to Micah for another reason. In spring he and his family celebrate the Jewish holiday of Passover or *Pesach* (PEH-sock). Passover begins each year on the fifteenth day of the month of *Nisan,* according to the Hebrew calendar, and lasts for seven or eight days. It celebrates an important event in Jewish history. More than three thousand years ago, the ancestors of the Jews, called the Israelites, were slaves in Egypt. With the help of God, they gained their freedom and their identity. Since that time, Jews all over the world have been celebrating Passover.

Before Passover begins, Micah, his brother, Jared, and his sister, Jenna, listen as their father reads about some of the traditions of Passover.

Passover, one of Judaism's most important holidays, begins with a ritual called a *seder* (SAY-duhr). Seder is a Hebrew word that means "order." The seder is a joyous celebration usually held at home. It includes blessings and prayers, chants and songs, as well as a delicious meal with many special foods.

The seder is held every year to help Jews remember the story of their ancestors' *exodus* (EX-uh-dus) from Egypt long ago. The story can be found in the book of Exodus in the Torah (toh-RAH), a sacred Jewish book. By celebrating Passover, Jews have the opportunity to participate in their history and be guided by its lessons.

The Passover Story

When famine came to Canaan, the land where the Israelites lived, many took refuge in Egypt. At first, their lives were happy. Over many hundreds of years, however, the Israelites grew in number. One day, a new Pharaoh (FAIR-oh), the Egyptian leader, began to fear the strength of the Israelites. He made them all into slaves, forcing them to work long hours at hard jobs with no pay. Even worse, each time a boy was born to an Israelite family, Pharaoh gave orders for the child to be put to death.

One Israelite woman had a son but kept him hidden away. Finally, when he was too big to disguise any longer, she made a basket of reeds. She put the baby inside and set it adrift in the Nile River. An Egyptian princess, who was bathing nearby, discovered the child. She took pity on him and brought him to the palace to be raised.

She gave the child the name Moses, which means "to draw up from the water." Although he grew up in the palace as an Egyptian, Moses knew the Israelites were his people. One day Moses saw an Egyptian beating a poor Israelite. He could not control his anger and killed the Egyptian. Then Moses had to flee for his life.

Moses became a shepherd. One day he watched as a bush burst into flames. Although the bush burned, its leaves stayed fresh and green. Curious, Moses approached the burning bush. It was then that he heard the voice of God. God commanded Moses to return to Egypt to lead his suffering people to a new land where they would once again be free and prosperous. God promised to help Moses.

So Moses came before Pharaoh and said, "Let my people go." Pharaoh, who did not believe in the God of Moses, answered, "Why should I let them go? I do not know your God or any reason I should obey the Lord."

He sent Moses away. Then he ordered the Israelites to work even harder. They had to make and carry bricks from dawn until dusk. The work was tiring, and as the Israelites stumbled under their heavy loads, the Egyptians beat them unmercifully.

Moses returned again and asked Pharaoh to release his people. Again Pharaoh refused. With God's help, Moses took his staff and turned the water in the river to blood to show the Egyptians the power of God. This was but the first of ten plagues that the Lord sent down upon the Egyptians.

When Pharaoh still refused to let the Israelites go, God sent a plague of frogs. They were leaping everywhere, and their croaking was deafening. Pharaoh said, "I will let your people go if you will only send the frogs away." But when Moses did as Pharaoh asked, the Egyptian leader went back on his word.

So God sent more plagues and turned the dust of the desert into lice. They covered the bodies of the Egyptians, biting them. God sent an illness that killed the cattle and horses. God sent flies buzzing into every Egyptian household. One day, the Egyptians woke to find themselves covered with boils. Still, Pharaoh did not want to free the Israelites. He turned Moses away each time he came to the palace to beg for the release of his people.

Next the Lord sent a violent hailstorm to ravage the Egyptian fields. Clouds of locusts darkened the sky. When they departed, the crops had been devoured. Then Moses stretched out his hand and God covered the land in darkness. For three days and three nights, there was no light. Still Pharaoh refused to give the Israelites their freedom.

Finally, God spoke to Moses. "I will send one more plague, worse than all the others. After that, I know Pharaoh will let you leave Egypt."

Moses told Pharaoh that an angel of the Lord would pass over Egypt and kill the firstborn son in every household.

God told Moses, "On the tenth day of this month, every family of Israel should bring a perfect lamb into their home. On the evening of the fourteenth day, the lamb should be killed and its blood smeared on the doorpost of the house."

On that night, Moses gave God's instructions to the Israelites and they followed them. They roasted the lamb and ate it, for it was the night of the Lord's passover. And God commanded them, "You shall keep this feast of the Passover forever, to remember how I brought you forth from the land of Egypt."

At midnight, the angel of death swept through Egypt and struck down the firstborn in every household. Only the Israelites, who had marked their doorposts with lamb's blood as the Passover sacrifice, were spared.

Pharaoh called Moses. He said, "Take your people away from my land. Go tonight. Your God is more powerful even than Pharaoh." And so the Israelites were freed from their bondage.

Quickly they gathered together all the possessions they could carry. Those who were making bread baked the dough without giving it time to rise. They had to leave right away, in case Pharaoh should change his mind.

For several days, the Israelites traveled across the desert until they came to the shores of the Red Sea. Then they heard the chariot wheels of Pharaoh's army approaching quickly. They realized that Pharaoh wanted to take them back to slavery. The Israelites were in despair.

Suddenly, God opened the waters of the sea. The waters divided and parted, allowing the Israelites to walk across on dry ground. Once they were safely on the other side, the sea flooded back. Pharaoh's army, which was following the Israelites, drowned.

The Israelites trusted in God and God helped to set them free. They gained their liberation from slavery on that day. The Passover seder celebrates that freedom.

The Haggadah

The readings, blessings, and songs for the celebration of Passover are found in a special book called the *Haggadah* (hah-GAH-dah). The name comes from a Hebrew word that means "to tell."

Long ago, Haggadot (hah-gah-DOTE) were written in Hebrew, the religious language of Jews. Today, most Haggadot include Hebrew and a translation. Micah's family uses a Haggadah that is printed in Hebrew and English. The translations make it easy for everyone to understand and participate in the seder.

Although most people follow the same general order during the seder, there is still a lot of room for creativity. Each family interprets the seder in their own way.

Most of the sacred books of Judaism, such as the Torah, have no illustrations or decoration. The Haggadah is one of the few Jewish texts that has artwork in it. Many Haggadot contain beautiful paintings of the Passover story.

Micah studies an ancient handwritten Haggadah during a visit to the Dalsheimer Rare Book Room in the Klau Library of the Hebrew Union College–Jewish Institute of Religion in Cincinnati. Before the invention of the printing press, Haggadot were written by hand and passed down from one generation to the next.

The Foods of Passover

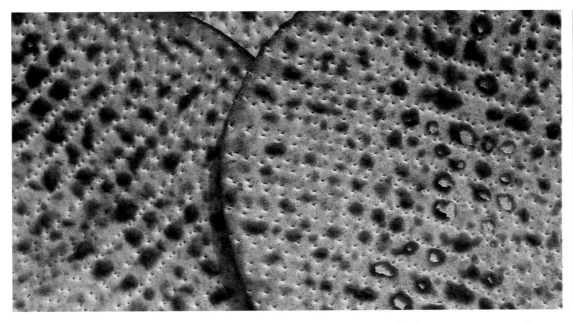

Since the very first Passover in Egypt, people have prepared special foods for the seder. Many people eat a roasted lamb as their ancestors did. A special kind of unleavened bread, called *matzah* (MAH-tzah), is one of the most important Passover foods.

Jews eat matzah during Passover because it is just like the unleavened bread their ancestors ate when they fled from Egypt. The Israelites had no time to let the dough rise as they normally would. They had to mix it, bake it quickly, and go.

Matzah is made from only two ingredients: water and flour. There are strict rules about the making of matzah for Passover. Only eighteen minutes may pass from the time that the water has been mixed with the flour, the dough has been rolled out, and the matzah has finished baking. That is because eighteen minutes is the time it takes for flour and water to start to ferment and the bread to rise.

People need lots of matzah for Passover. During the week of the Passover celebration, matzah replaces bread in Jewish homes. People find all sorts of ways to incorporate matzah in their diets. There are matzah sandwiches, and a breakfast favorite—*matzah brei* (MAH-tzah BRY), a dish made with matzah and scrambled eggs.

Matzah is made from wheat that is ground into flour and mixed with water. Long ago, people made matzah by hand. Today, however, most people buy it at a store that sells kosher foods.

9

Micah helps his grandmother, Bubby, get ready for the Passover meal. *Bubby* is a Yiddish word that means "grandmother." They make *haroset* (chah-ROH-set), one of the foods needed for the seder.

Haroset

3 apples, grated or
   chopped
1/2 cup pecans or
   walnuts, chopped
1 teaspoon sugar
a dash of cinnamon
1 tablespoon of kosher
   wine

Mix all the ingredients together in a bowl. Refrigerate until it is time to serve.

To celebrate Passover, Jewish families prepare many special foods. Some of these are symbolic and used only during the seder. Others are traditional foods eaten during the entire holiday. But all of them are prepared in a special way just for Passover.

At one time, all Jews believed it was important to eat only *kosher* (KOH-shur) foods. This is food prepared according to the laws of the Torah. Today, many Jewish families follow this custom during Passover. Micah's family serves kosher food at their Passover seder. Many supermarkets, as well as Jewish specialty stores, stock products that are labeled "Kosher for Passover."

At school during Passover week, Micah and his Jewish friends eat matzah for lunch. Their friends who are not Jewish enjoy tasting matzah.

Getting Ready

Before Passover begins, many Jewish households collect and get rid of all the bread, crackers, cookies, and other foods that have been made with yeast. Foods made with yeast are called *hametz* (chah-MAYTZ). This is a Hebrew word for "bread" in which flour and water have been allowed to ferment and rise. Many families make a game of this activity.

This tradition comes from a commandment in the Torah. By taking away all hametz and forbidding its use during Passover, matzah becomes that much more special.

(Above) Micah and Jared help get ready for Passover by collecting all the hametz that they can find.

(Right) On the night before Passover begins, Micah searches for the last few crumbs of hametz. He sweeps up the crumbs with a feather.

For days, everyone works hard to prepare for the seder. They search for hametz, they shop for kosher foods, they cook, and they clean. On the day of the seder, everyone dresses in their very best clothing.

The children help to set the table. They put out the best china, napkins, and silverware. Along with a plate of matzah, they place a special seder plate on the table. This plate contains small amounts of six different foods that symbolize the story of the Israelites' exodus from Egypt. At sundown on the first night of Passover, everyone is ready for the seder to begin.

(Above) Jared's mother helps him straighten his *yarmulke* (YAH-muh-kah). This is a head covering that people can wear to show respect and humility before God.

(Left) Micah brings in a plate of matzah while Jenna sets the table with the best dishes.

The Seder

The seder begins with the *Kadesh* (KAH-desh), a prayer to sanctify the day. Both of Micah's grandfathers take turns leading the ceremony, and everyone at the table has a part to play. The Jews celebrate Passover because the Torah commands them to do so.

> *You shall observe the Feast of Unleavened Bread,*
> *for on this very day I brought your ranks out of the land of Egypt;*
> *you shall observe this day throughout the generations*
> *as an institution for all time.*
>
> *Exodus 12:17*

In the course of the Passover seder, four cups of wine are drunk to commemorate each promise of liberation in the Torah. The first comes at the beginning of the seder and is called the *Kiddush* (KIH-dush).

Micah hands his grandmother a copy of the Haggadah. Micah's family has a Haggadah for each person at the seder so that they can read from it or just follow along.

14

Micah's grandfather, *Zayde* (ZAY-dee), begins the seder service by reading a prayer from the Haggadah.

I am the Lord.
I will free you from the
burdens of the Egyptians
and deliver you from
bondage.

Exodus 6:6

15

Passover is a special time for Micah's family because all the generations gather together. His grandparents have come all the way from Georgia to take part in the seder. For Micah's family, celebrating Passover is like being in a play. As they read the Passover story, each person tries to imagine what it was like to be a slave in Egypt.

The family dining room becomes a stage, the seder plate with its symbolic foods provides the props, and each member of the family is an actor. Reading from the Haggadah, they become slaves in Egypt, and experience for themselves the joy of God's redemption.

The Seder Plate

The Symbols of Passover

מָרוֹר
Maror
(mah-ROR)
Bitter herbs such as
horseradish—
a symbol of the
bitterness of slavery.

זְרוֹעַ
Zeroa
(zeh-ROH-ah)
A roasted lamb
shank bone—
a symbol of the
Passover sacrifice.

בֵּיצָה
Beitzah
(BAY-tzah)
A roasted egg—
a symbol of life.

פֶּסַח

Pesach
(PEH-sock)
Passover

כַּרְפַּס
Karpas
(KAHR-pahs)
A green, like parsley—
a symbol of rebirth
and spring.

חֲזֶרֶת
Hazaret
(chah-zeh-RET)
Chopped bitter herbs
like horseradish—
a symbol of the
bitterness of slavery.

חֲרֹסֶת
Haroset
(chah-ROH-set)
Chopped apples and nuts
mixed with wine—
a symbol of the mortar
the Israelite slaves made
for the bricks in Egypt.

19

Each person at the seder table dips a piece of parsley, or karpas, into saltwater before eating it.

Many of today's Passover traditions began thousands of years ago in the Middle East. Long ago, it was a custom of the ancient Greeks and Romans to dip their food before eating it, and the rich dined while reclining on pillows. Following these customs reminded Jews that they, too, were free. That is why during the seder, Jews dip their food. They also recline at the table. Today, this means simply leaning against a soft pillow in a chair. Although these customs may seem old-fashioned today, for many people they provide an important link with the past.

The first symbol from the seder plate is *karpas* (KAHR-pahs), or parsley. The parsley celebrates the life and rebirth of springtime. After a prayer, each person at the table takes a little piece of parsley and dips it into a bowl of saltwater before eating it. The saltwater symbolizes the tears that the Israelites shed when they were slaves in Egypt.

As the seder continues, Micah's grandfather takes the middle matzah from inside the matzah cover and breaks it in half. He puts one piece back into the cover between two other pieces of matzah. The other half becomes the *afikomen* (ah-fee-KOH-men). Micah's father hides it well somewhere in the house. Later, the children will search for it everywhere. The one who finds the afikomen can trade it for a prize or a gift. Tradition says that the seder cannot end until the afikomen has been found and redeemed.

Holding up a piece of matzah, the leader of the seder service says these words from the Haggadah:

> *This is the bread of affliction,*
> *the poor bread, which our ancestors ate in the land of Egypt.*
> *Let all who are hungry come eat.*
> *Let all who are in want share the hope of Passover.*

So begins the major part of the seder. Now, reading from the Haggadah, each person will hear the Passover story retold. Each person will taste the foods from the Passover plate and relive the exodus in his or her own imagination.

The afikomen is placed in its own special cover before it is hidden.

This is the bread of affliction ...

The Four Questions

After the tale of the Israelites' exodus from Egypt has been told, everyone at the seder table waits for the youngest child to ask the Four Questions. After asking the questions in English, Jared, who is the youngest child, sings the verses in Hebrew. *Ma nishtana* (MAH nish-TAH-nah), the first words that he sings, are Hebrew words that mean "Why is this night different from all other nights?"

Micah and Jenna help Jared ask the Four Questions.

Why is this night different from all other nights?

On all other nights we eat bread or matzah,
  on this night — only matzah.

On all other nights, we eat all kinds of herbs;
  on this night we especially eat bitter herbs.

On all other nights, we do not dip herbs at all;
  on this night we dip them twice.

On all other nights, we eat in an ordinary manner;
  tonight we dine with special ceremony.

Haggadah

The Torah teaches that the seder is a time for questions and a time for answers. One of the main reasons Passover is celebrated year after year after year in Jewish homes is so that each new generation can learn. It is a time for children to learn about their faith and their identity. Micah's father has started a special family tradition. His children can ask him anything they like during the seder, and he will gladly answer them.

As the seder continues, people are chosen to read the parts of the Four Children. In this section, the Haggadah tells about four different children: the Wise, the Wicked, the Simple, and the One Unable to Ask. Each different child hears the Passover story in a different way. The Haggadah emphasizes that there are many ways to learn about the word of God.

Passover also teaches an important lesson about compassion. When reading about the plagues that God sent to the Egyptians, the guests at the Passover meal take a drop of wine from the glass as each plague is mentioned. They spill the drop onto their plate. At the seder, wine is a symbol of happiness. By giving up a drop of it, they show that their happiness is diminished. This action symbolizes compassion for the Egyptians, who suffered greatly.

Jenna dips her finger in the wine and spills a drop.

Four times the Torah bids us tell our children of the Exodus from Egypt.
Four times the Torah repeats: "And you shall tell your child on that day..."
Haggadah

Micah and his father share a Hillel Sandwich.

An important part of the seder comes near the end of the readings when it is time to taste the *maror* (mah-ROR), or bitter herbs. Micah tries a little on a piece of matzah and makes an awful face. Maror is horseradish and tastes strong and bitter. Afterward, Micah's father shows him how to mix a bit of maror and a bit of haroset on a piece of matzah. This is called a Hillel Sandwich, after a great rabbi named Hillel. It represents the mixture of bitter with sweet that is so much a part of Passover.

Before the food is brought to the table, each person is offered a hard-boiled egg, the *beitzah* (BAY-tzah) of the seder plate. Like karpas, the beitzah represents spring and rebirth. Micah likes to dip his egg in saltwater before eating it because then it tastes even better.

25

The seder meal consists of many traditional foods such as *gefilte* (geh-FIL-teh) *fish* and matzah ball soup, Micah's favorite. There is also a chicken dish, stewed fruit, a Passover *kugel* (KOO-guhl), and, of course, a big bowl of haroset.

Searching for the Afikomen

He takes it to his father, who gives him a gift in exchange.

After everyone has eaten, it is time to search for the afikomen. The children spread out all over the house. They look under the furniture, up on the bookshelves, and inside the piano bench. Finally, Micah discovers it hidden behind a pillow on the couch.

Inside the box is a real silver dollar. Then Micah's father divides the afikomen into pieces and gives one to everyone at the table. They eat the afikomen at the very end of the seder, so that the taste of matzah will be the last thing they remember from the meal.

(Below) Jared places the Cup of Elijah on the table. This special goblet symbolizes the future redemption of the Jews, when the prophet Elijah will come again. During Passover, people usually set an extra place and have an extra chair at the table for Elijah, a symbolic guest at each Passover seder.

(Right) Micah opens the door for Elijah at the end of the seder.

28

Passover is a time of celebration and there are many wonderful Passover songs to express the joy of the occasion. Some come from Europe, and some from the Middle East. Some come from the United States. For example, the spiritual "Go Down Moses" tells the story of God's redemption of the Israelites in the land of Egypt. It is sung at Passover because of its theme of slavery and liberation.

One of Micah's favorites is a song called "Dayenu." This Hebrew phrase means "It would have been enough . . ."

A song of thanksgiving, the verses of "Dayenu" say: (1) If God had only brought us out of Egypt, it would have been enough. (2) If God had only given us the Sabbath, it would have been enough. (3) If God had only given us the Torah, it would have been enough.

Dayenu

I - lu ho - tzi ho - tzi - a - nu, ho - tzi - a - nu mi - mitz - ra - yim,

ho - tzi - a - nu mi - mitz - ra - yim da - yei - nu.

(Chorus) Da - da - yei - nu, ____ da - da - yei - nu, ____ da - da - yei - nu, da -

1, 2.
yei - nu da - yei - nu da - yei - nu.

3.
yei - nu da - yei - nu.

2. I-lu na-tan, na-tan la-nu, na-tan la-nu
et ha-sha-bat, na-tan la-nu et ha-sha-bat,
dayenu. (Chorus)

3. I-lu na-tan, na-tan, la-nu, na-tan la-nu
et ha-to-rah, na-tan la-nu et ha-to-rah,
dayenu. (Chorus)

After the Passover meal, it is time for dessert and singing. The end of the seder is marked by a reading of *Hallel* (HAH-lel), a collection of several psalms from the Bible. Everyone gives praise to God for past redemption and for freedom from slavery. Passover, the most celebrated holiday in Judaism, is a time for Jews all over the world to reflect on the distant past, experience the Passover story in the present, and look forward to a new redemption in the days to come.

The seder ends with singing and a spirit of joy.

Glossary

afikomen (ah-fee-KOH-men) A piece of matzah that is hidden away early in the Passover celebration. At the end, the children search for the afikomen, and hold it for ransom. The seder cannot end until the afikomen has been redeemed for a gift or prize.

beitzah (BAY-tzah) A roasted egg, one of the symbols on the seder plate, represents life, rebirth, and spring.

exodus (EX-uh-dus) A mass departure. This is the term used by the Israelites for their flight out of Egypt.

famine A time when people are hungry or starving because they cannot grow enough food.

gefilte fish (geh-FIL-teh fish) Traditional fish cakes served for Passover made from ground fish and matzah meal.

Haggadah (hah-GAH-dah) A special book, usually beautifully illustrated, that is used during Passover. It contains the religious service, prayers, and songs for the celebration. The plural is Haggadot (hah-gah-DOTE).

Hallel (HAH-lel) A collection of psalms read at the end of the seder.

hametz (chah-MAYTZ) Bread or any food made with yeast or allowed to ferment.

haroset (chah-ROH-set) A special food on the seder plate that symbolizes the mortar for the bricks that the Israelites used when they worked for Pharaoh during their enslavement.

hazaret (chah-zeh-RET) One of the symbols of the seder plate, consisting of chopped bitter herbs like horseradish that are eaten with matzah.

Kadesh (KAH-desh) A prayer to sanctify the day.

karpas (KAHR-pahs) A green, like parsley, that is one of the symbols on the seder plate. The parsley stands for spring and rebirth. People dip the parsley into saltwater before eating it.

Kiddush (KID-dush) A name for the first cup of wine shared during the seder.

kosher (KOH-shur) A term for food that has been prepared according to special laws in the Torah.

kugel (KOO-guhl) A dish made by baking noodles made with matzah flour, with raisins, and spices.

liberation Freedom.

ma nishtana (MAH nish-TAH-nah) A Hebrew phrase meaning "why is this night different from all other nights?"

maror (mah-ROR) Bitter herbs such as horseradish used on the seder plate as a symbol of the bitterness of slavery.

matzah (MAH-tzah) A crackerlike bread made from flour and water and baked quickly before any fermentation can occur. Matzah is a major symbol of the Passover celebration, which is also called the Feast of the Unleavened Bread or Feast of the Matzah.

matzah brei (MAH-tzah BRY) A dish served during Passover that combines scrambled eggs and matzah.

Moses The leader of the Israelites when they fled from Egypt and began their long journey to the Promised Land.

Nisan The seventh month in the Hebrew calendar.

Passover A week-long celebration of the Jewish faith that features a ceremonial dinner called a seder on the first two nights.

Pesach (PEH-sock) The Hebrew word for Passover.

Pharaoh (FAIR-oh) Leader of the Egyptians at the time when the Hebrews were enslaved in Egypt.

plagues A series of tragic events that happened to the Egyptians when Pharaoh refused God's command to let the Israelites go free.

redemption To be saved.

seder (SAY-duhr) A special ceremonial meal held on the first and second nights of the week-long Passover celebration. Seder means "order" in Hebrew, and the meal follows a traditional pattern that remains the same from year to year.

Torah (toh-RAH) A sacred book of the Jews, included as the first five books of the Bible: Genesis, Exodus, Leviticus, Numbers, and Deuteronomy.

unleavened A food that does not contain yeast or is not allowed to ferment and rise.

yarmulke (YAH-muh-kah) A small skull cap worn to show humility and respect before God.

zeroa (zeh-ROH-ah) A roasted shank bone from a lamb and a symbol of the Passover sacrifice. It is one of the symbols on the seder plate.

Index

Page numbers in italic type refer to illustrations.

Photo © J. Miles Wolf

The Plum Street Synagogue in Cincinnati was built in 1866. It is one of the oldest temples in the United States. A National Historic Landmark, it is also the home of American Reform Judaism, founded by Rabbi Isaac Mayer Wise.